JOHN HARBISON

FLASHES AND ILLUMINATIONS

for Baritone and Piano

AMP 8137

First printing: January 2000

ISBN 0-7935-9202-X

Associated Music Publishers, Inc.

DISTRIBUTED BY

HAL•LEONARD®
CORPORATION

7777 W. BLUEMOUND RD. P.O. BOX 13819 MILWAUKEE, WI 53213

PROGRAM NOTE

Flashes and Illuminations (1994) was commissioned by Reader's Digest / Meet the Composer for baritone Sanford Sylvan and pianist David Breitman. Honoring their long musical partnership, I composed a piece that falls equally to pianist and singer, from poets who invite sustained reflection.

The title comes, in part, from the "Flashes and Dedications" section of Eugenio Montale's book *La Bufera* (The Storm), in which the poem "Sulla Greve" appears (the Greve is a small river near Florence). For Montale, the "flash" is a momentary perception of the natural world or a human interaction that brings sudden insight.

Each poem suggested to me a Montalean flash: sudden, muted lightning on the horizon.

—JOHN HARBISON

The premiere performance of Flashes and Illuminations
*was given by Sanford Sylvan, baritone, and David Breitman, piano
at Emmanuel Church, Boston, March 2, 1996*

duration: ca. 15 minutes

for Sanford Sylvan and David Breitman

FLASHES AND ILLUMINATIONS

I. On the Greve

Eugenio Montale
(translated by John Harbison)

John Harbison

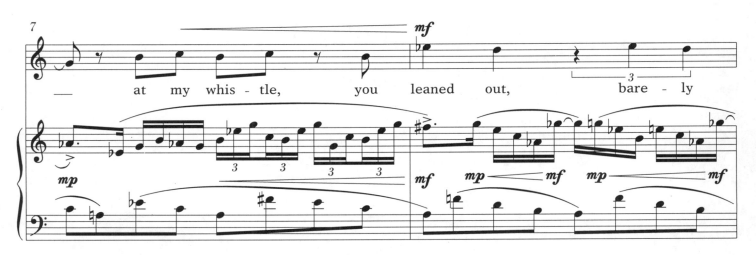

at my whis - tle, you leaned out, bare - ly

vis - i - ble. A rock, a

blocked fur - row, the swal - - low's black _____ flight, _____

a cov'r - ing for the world...

And now for me,

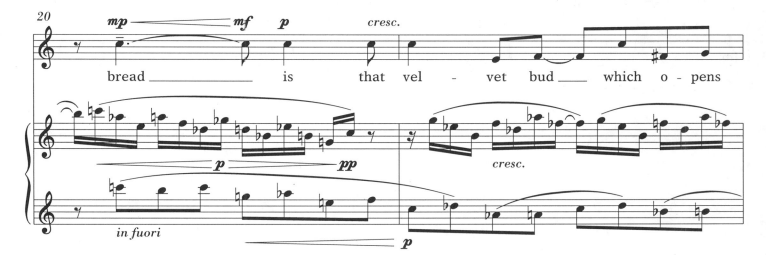

bread _____ is that vel - vet bud ____ which o - pens

un - clos - ing with a slide from a

man - do-lin,

4

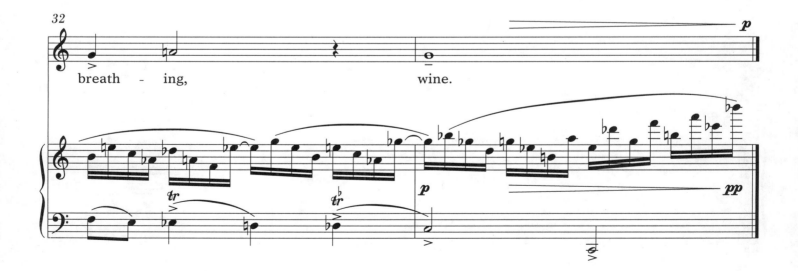

II. Chemin de Fer*

Elizabeth Bishop

Con moto ♩. = 69

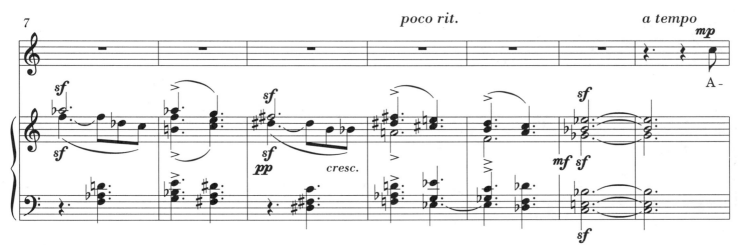

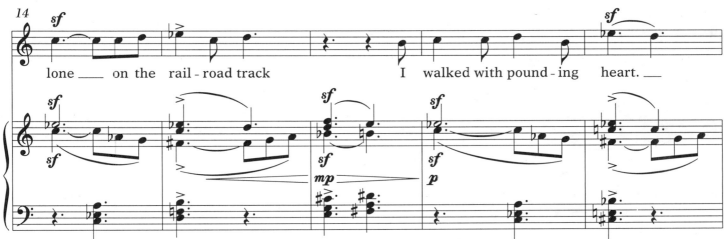

lone ___ on the rail - road track   I walked with pound - ing   heart. ___

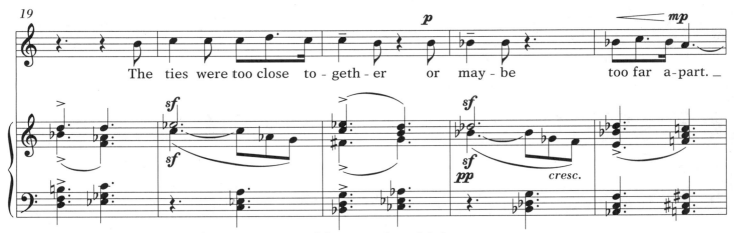

The ties were too close to - geth - er   or may - be   too far a - part. ___

* This song is also printed on page 25, transposed down a minor third.

The scen-'ry __ was im-pov-'rished: scrub pine __ and oak; __ be-yond __ its min-gled gray - green fo-liage I saw __ the lit-tle pond where the dirt-y her-mit lives, lie __ like an old tear __ hold-ing on-to its

in - ju-ries   lu - cid-ly   year _____ af - ter

Poco più mosso

year. _____ The her-mit shot off his shot - gun and the

tree _____ by his cab - in shook.

O - ver the pond _____ went a rip - ple.

* *ossia: omit L.H. upper note*

The pet hen went
chook-chook.

"Love _____ should be put _____ in - to ac - tion!"

screamed _____ the old her-mit.

A-cross the pond _____ an ech - o

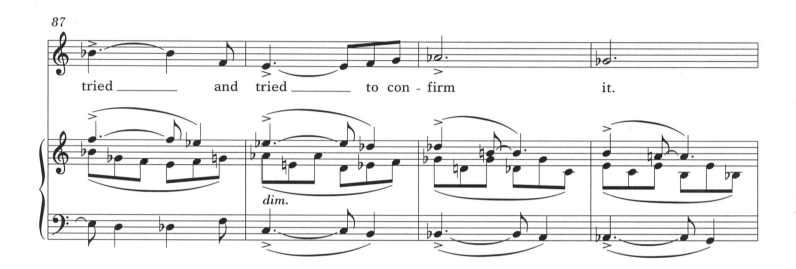

tried _____ and tried _____ to con - firm it.

molto rit. al fine

dim. al fine

(rit.)

(dim.)

morendo

III. The Winds of Dawn*

Michael Fried

* This song is also printed on page 30, transposed down a minor third.

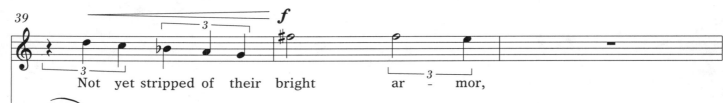

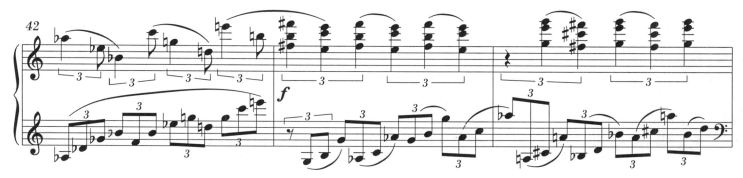

I am at last the war-ri-or I have al-ways want-ed to

be.

IV. Cirque d'Hiver

Elizabeth Bishop

back. _____ She stands up-on her toes and turns and turns. A

slant-ing spray ___ of ar-ti-fi-cial ros - es _____ is stitched a-cross her skirt and tin-sel

bod - - ice. A-bove her head ___ she pos - es an-oth-er spray ____ of

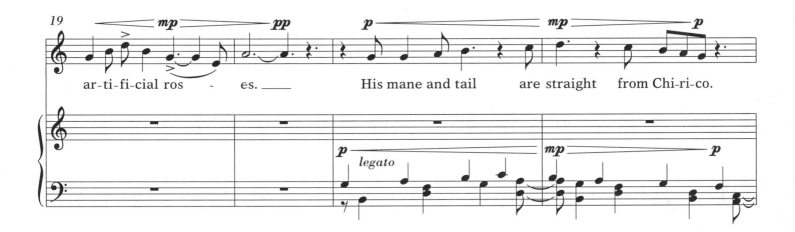

ar-ti-fi-cial ros - es. ___ His mane and tail are straight from Chi-ri-co.

He has a for - mal, mel-an-chol-y soul. He feels her pink toes

dan-gle t'ward _ his back a - long _____ the lit - tle

pole _____ that pierc - es both her

bod-y _____ and her soul and goes through his, and

V. To Be Recited to Flossie on Her Birthday

William Carlos Williams

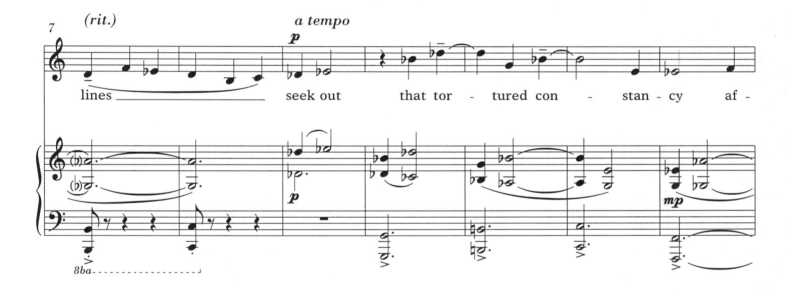

Let him who may a - mong the con - tin - u - ing lines _____ seek out that tor - tured con - stan - cy af -

firms _ where I _ per - sist _____ let me say a -

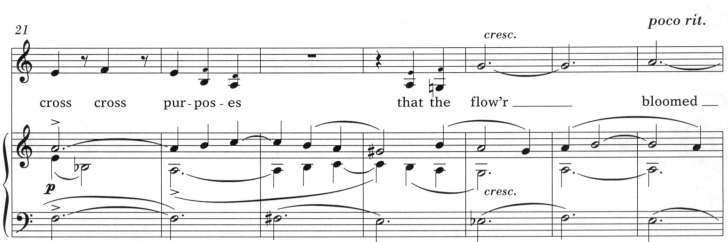

cross cross pur-pos-es that the flow'r _____ bloomed __

__ strug-gling to as - sert it-self sim-ply un-der the con-flict -

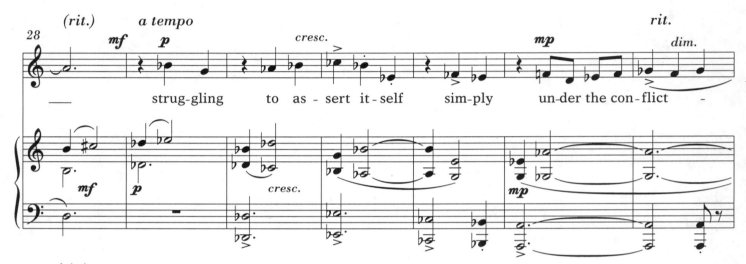

- - ing lights _____ you will be - lieve me a rose ____

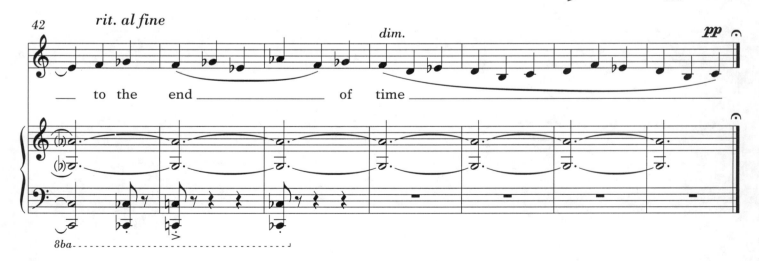

__ to the end _____ of time _____

VI. December 1

Czeslaw Milosz

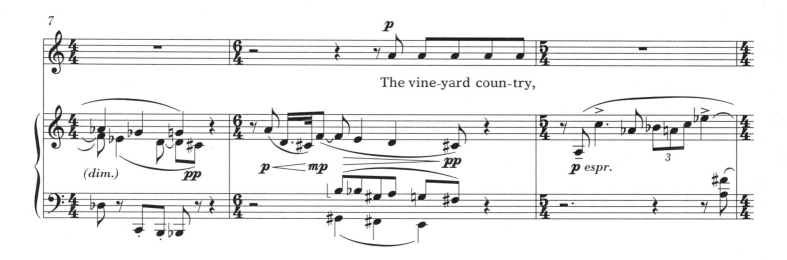

The vine-yard coun-try,

rus-set,   red-dish,   car-mine-brown _ in this sea - son. _

in a pool sur-round-ed by trees.

Dark red-woods, trans-par-ent pale-leaved birch-es. _

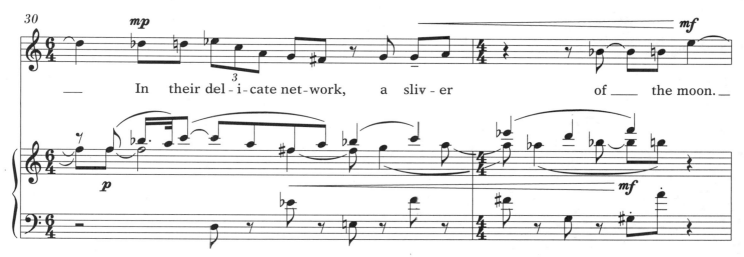

_ In their del-i-cate net-work, a sliv-er of __ the moon. _

transposed down a minor third

II. Chemin de Fer

Elizabeth Bishop

lone ___ on the rail-road track   I   walked with pound-ing   heart. ___

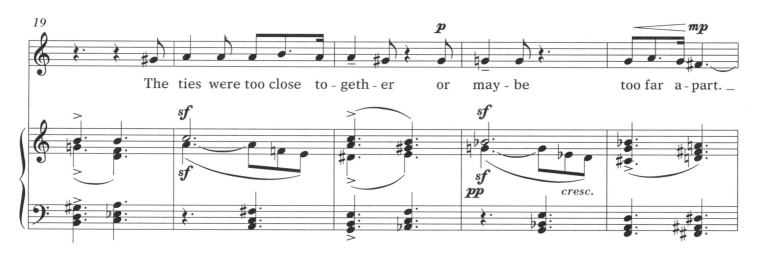

The ties were too close to-geth-er   or   may-be   too far a-part. _

* ossia: omit L.H. upper note

28

The pet hen went

dim.

mf

chook-chook.

mp

sf

f sf

sf

f sf

"Love ____ should be put ____ in - to ac - tion!"

sf

sf martellato

sf

Ped. molto

sf

ff

screamed _____ the old her-mit.

sf

sf

A-cross the pond _____ an ech - o

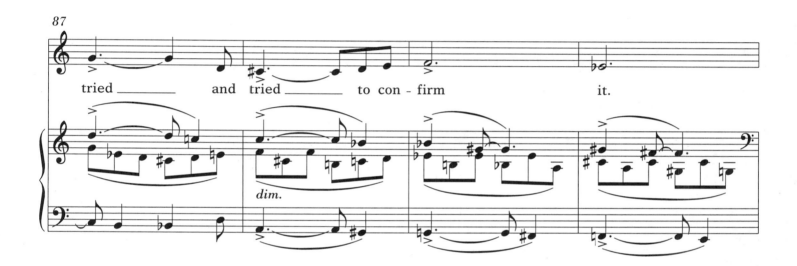

tried _____ and tried _____ to con - firm it.

molto rit. al fine

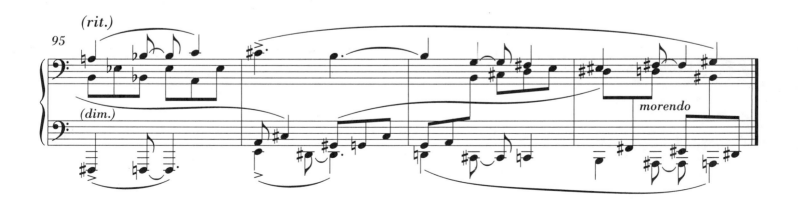

transposed down a minor third

III. The Winds of Dawn

Michael Fried

Tumultuoso ♩ = 160

dawn an - swer those ques - tions As ____

____ it may, ____ let the

winds ___ of dawn _____ lev - el their fierce gusts A-cross the

reek - ing black - - ness Un-til all is

swept a-way.

In my dream,

o - ver-look-ing a plain of slaugh-tered bod - ies

Not yet stripped of their bright ar - mor,

I am at last the war - ri - or I have al - ways want-ed to

be.